A WHALE IS NOT A FISH

and Other Animal Mix-ups

by Melvin Berger

Illustrated by Marshall Peck III

SCHOLASTIC INC.

NEW YORK   TORONTO   LONDON   AUCKLAND   SYDNEY

For Jake
with love
—M.B.

For Robin
—M.H.P. III

ISBN 0-590-47477-4

Text copyright © 1995 by Melvin H. and Gilda Berger Trust.
Illustrations copyright © 1995 by Scholastic Inc.
All rights reserved. Published by Scholastic Inc.

16 15 14 13   2 3 4 5 6/0

Printed in the U.S.A.   23

First printing, September 1995

Book and cover design by Laurie Williams

Contents

A Whale Is Not a Fish

Whales and fish live in the water. They both have stream-lined bodies. But —

Whales are immense. . . .

Whales range from big to gigantic. In fact, the blue whale is the largest animal that has ever lived. A full-grown blue whale is about as long as three buses, as heavy as 25 elephants, and as tall as a two-story house!

BLUE WHALE

. . . Fish are smaller.

Fish come in all sizes. Most are very much smaller than whales. The smallest fish of all is a goby. It is less than a half-inch long! The largest fish, though, are the size of small whales.

OKINAWAN GOBY with blue whale

Whales have sideways tail fins. . . .

The whale's fins are sometimes called flukes. When swimming, the whale swings its fins up and down. The moving fins push the whale forward in the water. Most whales cruise along at about four miles an hour. But when they are in a hurry, some whales can reach 35 miles an hour!

Whale skins are smooth and rubbery. . . .

Have you ever touched a whale? If you did, you would know that its skin feels very smooth. Petting a whale feels like rubbing your hand on a big balloon. Beneath the whale's skin is a layer of fat. It is called blubber. Some whales have blubber that is over one foot thick!

. . . Fish fins are straight up and down.

When swimming, the fish swings its fins from side to side. The tuna is one of the fastest swimmers in the ocean. It can zip along at about 45 miles an hour!

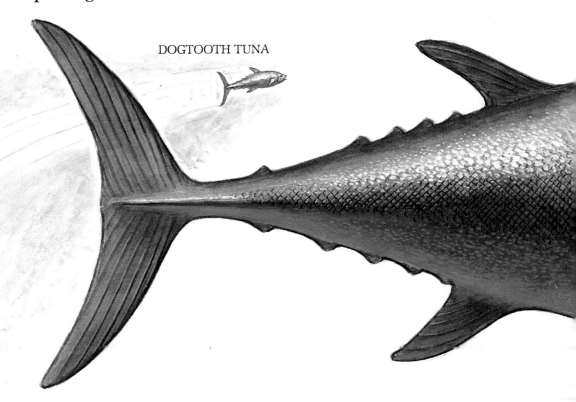

DOGTOOTH TUNA

. . . Fish are covered with thin, bony scales.

It's very different to pet a fish. Some scales feel smooth. But many feel sharp and rough. The sharpest ones are shark scales. They stick up like a layer of pointy nails!

Whales breathe air. . . .

Whales live in the water, but breathe oxygen from the air. Their nostrils, called blowholes, are at the top of the whale's head. They take immense breaths of air that fill their lungs. Some whales can then stay under the water for up to two hours without breathing! When they breathe out, they form a big spout of air and water.

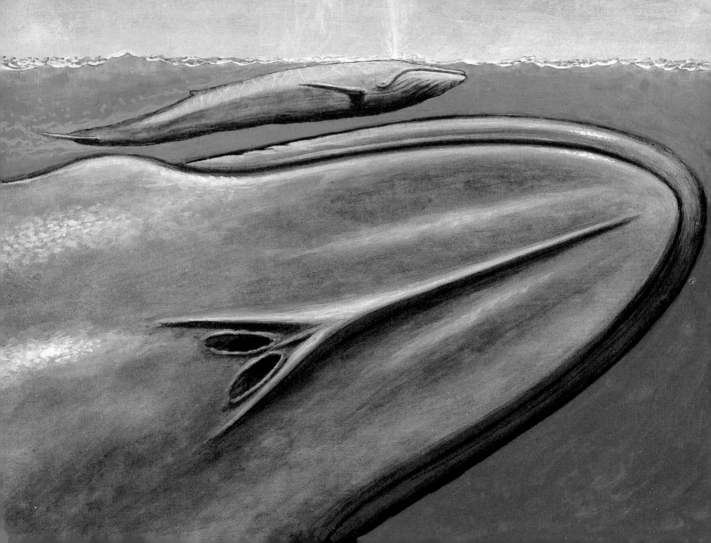

. . . Fish breathe water.

Fish also need oxygen. But they get it from the oxygen that is dissolved in the water. Fish take in water through the mouth. Then they force the water out through openings behind the head. These openings are called gills. The gills remove the dissolved oxygen from the water.

SWEETLIPS

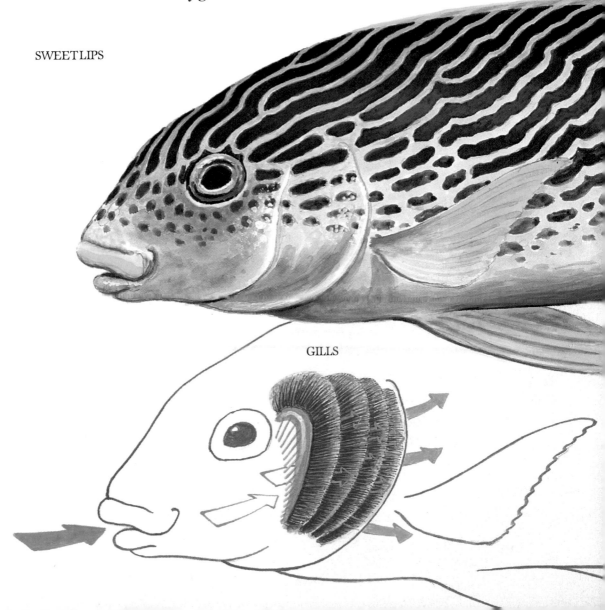

GILLS

Whales bear their young alive. . . .

Mother whales give birth to one baby whale at a time. But the baby can be huge. A baby blue whale weighs about 4,000 pounds — more than 500 human babies! The mother whale takes care of the baby for up to a year. She feeds it milk from her body. The baby whale gains about 200 pounds a day in the first seven months.

SPERM WHALE

Whales are warm-blooded. . . .

The whale's body temperature never changes. Most whales spend part of the year in the cold waters near the north and south poles. Then they head toward warmer seas. Yet, no matter how cold or warm the water, the whale's temperature stays the same.

. . . Most fish lay eggs.

Mother fish lay lots and lots of eggs in the water. In a couple of months the eggs hatch into baby fish. Sometimes the mother — or father — fish takes care of the babies. But most of the time the baby fish are on their own from the moment they are born.

PUMPKINSEED

. . . Fish are cold-blooded.

Cold-blooded is the opposite of warm-blooded. When fish swim in cold water, their bodies are cold. When they swim in warm water, their bodies are warm. Fish can adjust only to small and gradual changes of water temperature.

An Ape Is Not a Monkey

Apes and monkeys are hairy animals that live in jungles. Their faces often look similar. But —

Apes don't have tails. . . .

Apes — such as chimpanzees, gibbons, gorillas, and orangutans — mostly walk on the ground or climb in trees on two legs. Tails are of little use to them.

ORANGUTAN

GORILLA

Apes' arms are longer than their legs. . . .

Apes lean over as they walk. They lean forward on their fists. Because their arms are longer, apes walk nearly upright.

. . . Monkeys have tails.

Monkeys spend most of their time swinging through trees. They need the tail to keep their balance. Monkeys also use the tail as a brake. It slows them down as they leap from branch to branch. Some even use the tail to grab on to branches and vines.

RHESUS MONKEY

. . . Monkeys' arms and legs are about the same length.

Monkeys walk on all fours. Arms and legs of the same length are best for scampering through trees and along the ground.

Apes are big. . . .

A large body helps to protect the apes. Who would want to start a fight with an animal that is six feet tall and weighs 450 pounds? That's the size of an adult male gorilla.

GORILLA

. . . Monkeys are smaller.

Small bodies help monkeys get along. Most monkeys are light enough to sit on thin branches. And they are small enough to squeeze through the narrow spaces between branches. The smallest monkey is the pygmy marmoset. It is about six inches long and weighs less than a half pound!

PYGMY MARMOSET

Apes are very smart. . . .

Apes have large brains. They are among the most intelligent of all animals. Chimpanzees are smart enough to make "tools" of sticks to get at hard-to-reach food. Some chimps and gorillas have even learned to communicate with humans by sign language!

CHIMPANZEE

. . . Monkeys are less smart.

Monkeys are quite intelligent. It takes a good brain to judge distances when jumping from tree to tree. But monkeys are not nearly as smart as apes.

A Toad Is Not a Frog

Toads and frogs are small animals that live part of the time on land and part of the time in water. Such animals are called amphibians. Both toads and frogs have four legs, no tail, and bulging eyes. But —

Toads have dark, dry skins. . . .

Most toads are dull brown or gray in color. Their skin feels dry and rough. It is covered with bumps and warts. Some people believe that humans get warts when they touch a toad. That is *not* true.

GRAY TOAD

Toads spend more time on land. . . .

Toads hatch from eggs laid in the water. Then they swim about in the water as tadpoles. But once they become adult toads, they move to the land. From then on, they mostly live on land. You seldom see a toad on hot, sunny days. They are most active at night or on rainy days.

...Frogs have brighter, wet skins.

Most frogs are much more colorful than toads. A frog's skin feels moist all the time.

BULLFROG

...Frogs divide their time between land and water.

Frogs are also born from eggs and start life as tadpoles in the water. But most adult frogs spend as much time in water as on land. Some live in burrows under the ground. They leave their burrows only during or after a rainfall. The mistaken idea that frogs fall from the sky during the rain comes from this fact.

Toads' back legs are not big and strong. . . .

Toads mostly crawl about on land. They don't need very strong back legs to be able to crawl.

Toads have no teeth. . . .

Since they don't have teeth, toads swallow their food in one piece. Their favorite foods are insects, worms, and spiders.

. . . Frogs have big, strong back legs.

Frogs are jumpers. They depend on their powerful back legs for leaping great distances on land. The record for the longest frog jump is over 21 feet! Compare that with the human record — which is only eight feet longer. In water, a frog's webbed toes help it to swim very fast.

. . . Most frogs have teeth just in their upper jaws.

Frogs can't chew their meals, either. But a frog has a strange way of swallowing. The frog pulls its eyes down into its head. This helps to push the insect or small animal into its throat!

An Alligator Is Not a Crocodile

Alligators and crocodiles are almost look-alikes. Both have narrow bodies, rough skin, short legs, and long tails. But —

The alligator's snout is wide. . . .

The tip of the alligator's snout is broad and round. The alligator's powerful jaws can bite through a heavy wooden board. Yet they can be kept shut by a person's hands!

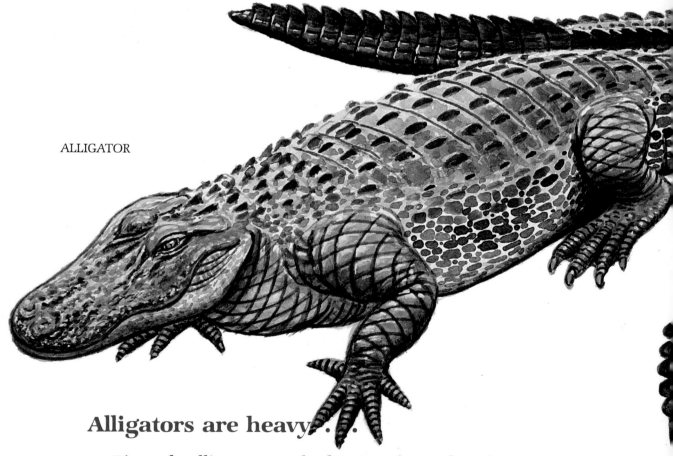

ALLIGATOR

Alligators are heavy. . . .

Big male alligators reach about 12 feet in length. They weigh up to 550 pounds.

. . . The crocodile's snout comes more to a point.

The crocodile has a smaller snout than the alligator. But most people fear the crocodile more than its look-alike. The crocodile is more likely to attack a person than an alligator is.

CROCODILE

. . . Crocodiles are lighter.

Big male crocodiles are as long as big male alligators. But they weigh only about 400 pounds.

Alligators are slow. . . .

Alligators mostly rest in the water. They wait for a fish, snake, frog, or turtle to come along. Then they grab the prey, pull it under the water, and eat it.

All of the alligator's teeth fit into its mouth. . . .

When the alligator closes its mouth, none of its teeth show. Yet in its mouth are many big, sharp teeth. They can rip right through an animal's flesh.

. . . Crocodiles are faster.

Crocodiles eat the same food as alligators. But crocodiles don't just sit and wait for their next meal. They slither around looking for animals to catch and eat.

. . . Two crocodile teeth show outside its mouth.

When the crocodile closes its mouth, an extra-long tooth on each side pokes outside its upper jaw.

A Bat Is Not a Bird

Bats and birds both have wings and can fly. They both live all over the world. But —

Bats are covered with fur. . . .

Most bats have brown, gray, or red fur everywhere but on the wings. A bat's wing is covered with smooth skin.

BROWN BAT

A bat's head looks like a tiny dog's head. . . .

Most bats have long snouts. They look like very small dogs or bears. Some bats, though, have flattened snouts.

. . . Birds are covered with feathers.

Birds have feathers everywhere except for the bill and feet. Feathers help birds to fly and keep a steady body temperature. They are the only animals with feathers.

SWALLOW

. . . Birds' heads are more rounded.

Most birds have rounded heads, even though the shape may be hidden by feathers.

Most bats have small, sharp teeth. . . .

Bats chew their food with their teeth. They chew very fast and digest their food quickly. Most prefer insects. Some eat scorpions or small mice. Vampire bats feed on animal blood, mostly the blood of cattle.

. . . Birds have bills.

Instead of teeth, birds have bills. The shape of the bill depends on the kind of food the bird eats. Woodpeckers use their sharp, pointed bills to poke into trees and find insects. Finches crack open hard seeds with their short, strong bills. And pelicans scoop up fish from the water in their long bills.

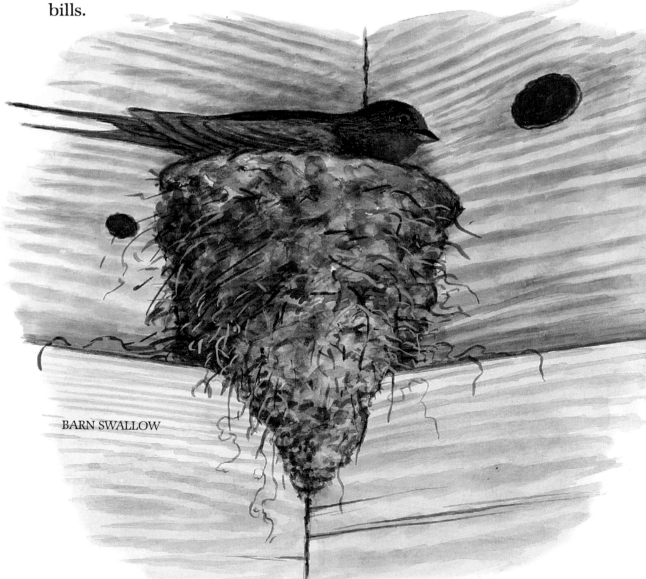

BARN SWALLOW

Bats bear their young alive. . . .

Bat mothers usually give birth to one baby at a time. The mother bat feeds the baby with milk from her body. Because bats do not build nests, the baby holds on to its mother for many weeks.

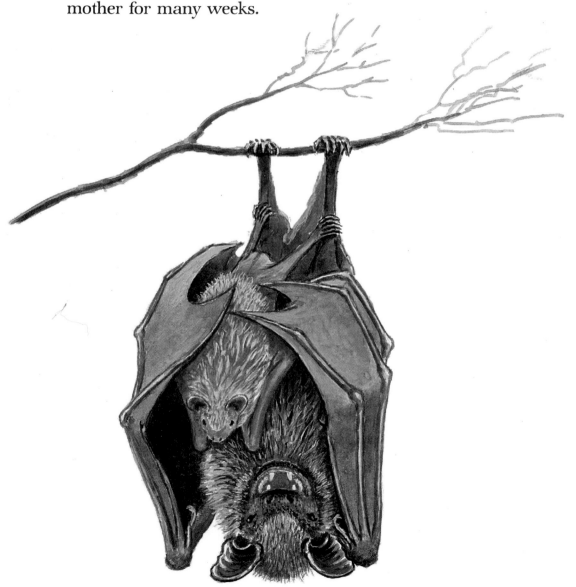

. . . Birds lay eggs.

Nearly all bird mothers lay eggs in nests. The mother or father keeps the eggs warm. After several weeks, the eggs hatch. The baby birds break open the eggs and squeeze out.

LARK

Bats have very good hearing

Bats fly mostly at night when it's hard to see. They make short, high, squeaky sounds and listen for the echoes. If it takes a long time to hear the echo, there is nothing nearby to bounce back the sound. A quick echo tells the bat that it is close to something — perhaps an insect, its favorite food.

. . . Birds have very good vision.

Most birds sleep at night and fly during the day. They usually depend more on sight than hearing to find something to eat. Birds have a very good sense of vision. An eagle can spot a mouse from a mile away! And with eyes on the sides of their heads, birds can see in almost every direction.

BROAD WINGED HAWK

A Moth Is Not a Butterfly

Moths and butterflies are insects. They are probably the most beautiful of all insects. But —

The moth's wings are connected. . . .

Moths have two sets of wings — a pair of front wings and a pair of back wings. The moth's front and back wings are hooked together.

TIGER MOTH

A moth at rest holds its wings flat. . . .

When a moth lands, it spreads its wings out level.

. . . The butterfly's wings are separate.

Butterflies also have two sets of wings. But the front and back wings are not attached to each other.

MONARCH BUTTERFLY

. . . A butterfly at rest holds its wings upright.

When a butterfly lands, its wings stand straight up like sails on a sailboat. The wings of both moths and butterflies are covered with fine, powdery scales. These scales catch the light and give the wings their pretty colors.

Most moths fly at dusk and at night. . . .

Moths usually hide during the day. That's how they keep safe from their daytime enemies. When flying, they look for the flower nectar and juice from fruit they like to drink.

POLYPHEMUS MOTHS

. . . Butterflies fly during the day.

Butterflies are not afraid to fly when the sun is shining. Many butterflies have a terrible taste. Animals that eat them by mistake learn to stay away from them. The butterfly's bright colors act as a warning.

HAIRSTREAK

METALMARK

GIANT SULPHUR

ALFALFA

Moths have fat, furry bodies. . . .

Moth bodies are large and covered with short hairs.

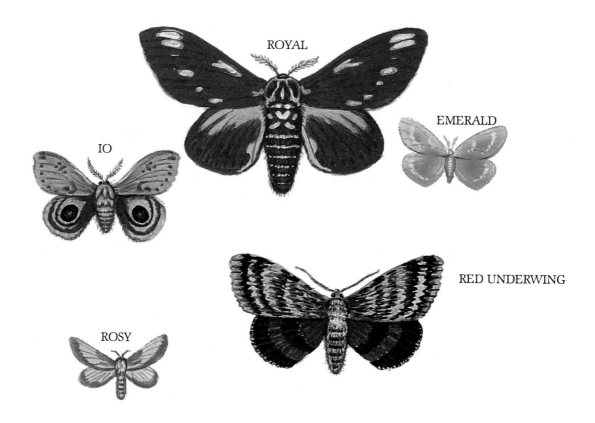

Moths have feathery antennae. . . .

Antennae are the long feelers on the heads of both moths and butterflies. They are mostly used for picking up odors. A moth's antennae look like fuzzy little feathers.

... Butterflies have thin, bare bodies.

Butterfly bodies are narrow and hairless.

DOGFACE

SKIPPER

COPPER

SILVERY BLUE

BUCKEYE

SWALLOWTAIL

... Butterflies have thin antennae.

Butterflies' antennae are also for smelling, and for hearing and touching, too. But butterflies' antennae look like thin, straight rods with knobs at the ends.

Some moth caterpillars produce silk. . . .

At one point in its life, a moth caterpillar spins a shell around itself. This shell is called a cocoon. The cocoon is made of one long thread. Silk is made from the cocoon of one kind of moth caterpillar. The caterpillar is called a silkworm. Silk is one of the strongest and most beautiful of all fibers.

SILKWORM

Moth caterpillars make holes in woolen clothing. . . .

Moths and butterflies grow from eggs into caterpillars. Then they grow into adult moths and adult butterflies. All caterpillars eat plant leaves. But moth caterpillars also eat wool. Moth caterpillars are to blame for the holes you sometimes find in your woolen clothes.

. . . Butterfly caterpillars produce silk, but it can't be used.

Butterfly caterpillars also spin cocoons of silk. But no one has found a way to unwind the thread and make it into silk fiber.

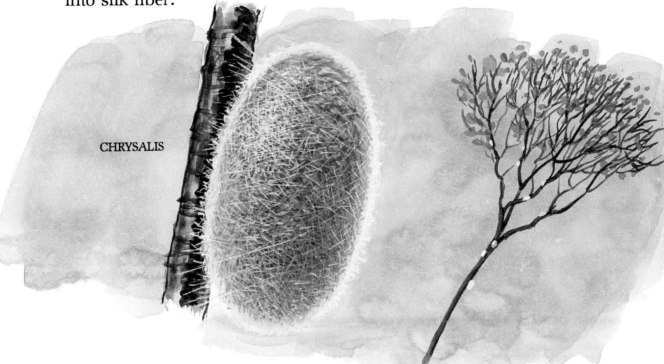

CHRYSALIS

. . . Butterfly caterpillars don't eat wool.

Butterfly caterpillars mostly eat green plants. They have no appetite for wool. So don't blame a butterfly for the hole in your favorite wool sweater.

A Hare Is Not a Rabbit

Hares and rabbits are small furry animals with long ears and short, fluffy tails. They scamper through gardens, fields, and woods. But —

Most hares are big. . . .

The biggest hares are 27 inches long. They weigh over eight pounds. Some of the biggest hares are called jackrabbits — even though they really are hares. The smaller snowshoe rabbits are also hares.

JACKRABBIT

Hares escape enemies by hopping away. . . .

When a hare senses danger, it leaps away on its powerful hind legs. Some hares reach speeds of up to 50 miles an hour!

. . . Rabbits are smaller.

The biggest rabbits are only about half as long as hares. And most rabbits weigh less than five pounds.

COTTONTAIL

. . . Rabbits would rather hide.

Rabbits can also jump great distances. But they prefer to hide from their enemies, rather than risk being caught. If an enemy gets too close, though, they do run. A rabbit's top speed is about 18 miles an hour.

Hares are born with fur and with eyes open. . . .

Mother hares give birth in a scratched-out hole in the ground. The newborns are ready to hop away a few hours later.

. . . Rabbits are born without fur and with eyes closed.

Mother rabbits give birth in shallow nests that they dig in the ground. They line the nests with grass and tufts of their own fur. Rabbit babies are born blind, without fur, and unable to hop. The mother rabbit cares for them for about two weeks, until they are able to see, they grow fur, and they can scamper away.

A Spider Is Not an Insect

Spiders and insects are bugs. Most bugs are tiny animals that bite us, scare us, and pester us during picnics. But —

Spiders have eight legs. . . .

All spiders have eight legs — four on each side. When spiders walk they move legs one and three on one side and legs two and four on the other side. For the next step they reverse — legs two and four on one side, one and three on the other.

ORB SPIDER

A spider's body has two main parts. . . .

The front part of the spider's body contains its head and thorax, or chest. A very thin waist separates the front part from the back. The back part is the abdomen, or belly. All spiders have two-part bodies. But they come in all sizes — from the big tarantula (10 inches long) to the tiny comb-footed spider (1/50th of an inch long).

. . . Insects have only six legs.

All insects have only six legs — three on each side. When insects walk, they move the middle leg on one side and the front and back legs on the other side. For the next step they reverse — front and back on one side, middle leg on the other.

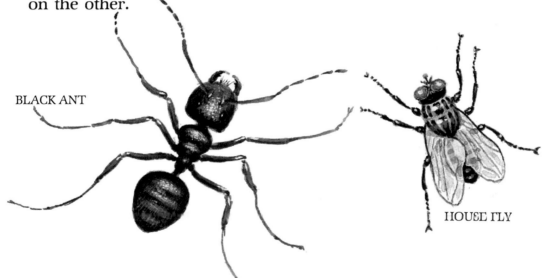

BLACK ANT

HOUSE FLY

. . . An insect's body has three main parts.

The bodies of insects — such as flies, ants, and bees — have three separate parts: head, thorax, and abdomen.

Spiders don't have wings. . . .

Spiders can crawl. Some can jump. But none of them can fly.

TARANTULA

Spiders don't have antennae. . . .

Insects have senses of touch and smell on their antennae. Spiders have these senses in their legs. Spider legs are covered with short bristles. These bristles feel things, pick up odors, and even "hear" sounds!

. . . Most insects have wings.

Most insects can fly. The common ant doesn't have wings. But many different kinds of ants do have wings.

POLYPHEMUS MOTH

. . . Most insects have antennae.

Almost all insects have a pair of antennae. The antennae give insects their senses of touch and smell. These senses are quite amazing. For example, male moths can smell females that are more than a mile away!

Crabs, shrimp, and lobsters are other animals with antennae.

Spiders wait for their food to come to them. . . .

Most spiders spin webs. Then they sit and wait. Sooner or later an insect gets trapped in the web. The spider pounces and makes a meal of the insect. Spiders kill the insects with their poison fangs. But only a few kinds of spiders are poisonous to humans.

GRASS SPIDER

. . . Insects look for their food.

Insects are always on the go. They move about looking for food. Insects eat almost anything, from plants to garbage, from dead animals to human blood.

PRAYING MANTIS

A Donkey Is Not a Mule

Donkeys and mules look like small horses. They can pull wagons and carry loads. But —

A donkey's parents are a male donkey and a female donkey. . . .

When male and female donkeys mate, they produce baby donkeys. The baby donkey grows up to look like a zebra without stripes. It has long ears, small feet, and long hairs at the end of its tail.

. . . **A mule's parents are a male donkey and a female horse.**

When a mule grows up, it is like a donkey in some ways and like a horse in other ways. But mules cannot usually have babies.

DONKEY, MULE, HORSE

Donkeys are small. . . .

Donkeys are usually between three and four feet tall at the shoulders. People use smaller donkeys for riding. They use larger donkeys to pull carts or carry loads.

Donkeys can be hard to handle. . . .

If donkeys are badly treated, they become very stubborn. Sometimes they refuse to move.

...Mules are bigger.

Most mules are bigger and stronger than donkeys. They are, more or less, five feet tall at the shoulders. In the past almost all farmers and miners used mules to bear heavy burdens.

...Mules are easier to work with.

Mules will keep on working even when treated badly. Also, it's easier to put a saddle on a mule than on a donkey. But sometimes mules will not do what they are asked. That's why we say some people are "as stubborn as a mule!"

A Porpoise Is Not a Dolphin

Porpoises and dolphins are both large, sleek-looking sea animals. They are related to the whale. But —

Porpoises are smaller. . . .

Porpoises measure up to about six feet in length and weigh no more than 220 pounds.

HARBOR PORPOISE

Porpoises have rounded snouts. . . .

The porpoise snout is blunt and round.

. . . Dolphins are larger.

Dolphins grow up to 13 feet long and can weigh about 600 pounds. The very largest dolphins are called killer whales — even though they are not whales. Killer whales can be 30 feet long and weigh ten tons!

BOTTLENOSE DOLPHIN

. . . Dolphins have pointed snouts.

The dolphin's snout looks more like a bird's beak. Also, the dolphin's head slopes down sharply to its beak.

58

Porpoise teeth are shaped like spades. . . .

The porpoise's teeth are flat at the bottom. But porpoises don't chew their food. They use their teeth to grab the small fish they eat. Then they swallow the fish whole.

SPECTACLED PORPOISE

Porpoises are slow swimmers. . . .

Porpoises can swim at speeds of about 12 miles per hour. They mostly swim close to ocean coasts.

. . . Dolphin teeth are pointed.

The dolphin's teeth look like the bottoms of ice-cream cones. Dolphins eat much the same food as porpoises. And they don't chew their food, either.

. . . Dolphins are faster swimmers.

Some dolphins can swim more than twice as fast as porpoises. They sometimes top 25 miles an hour. But they can keep up this speed only for a short time. Most dolphins swim in the salt water of the ocean. A few dolphins, though, swim in the fresh waters of large rivers and lakes in Asia and South America.

A Hedgehog Is Not a Porcupine

Hedgehogs and porcupines are covered with sharp spurs. Both use the spurs to protect themselves. But —

A hedgehog rolls into a ball when attacked. . . .

The hedgehog has one-inch-long, sharp spines all over its body. Just let an enemy come close. The hedgehog rolls into a ball with its spines sticking out. Now the hedgehog is safe from most attackers.

HEDGEHOG

. . . A porcupine goes after any attackers with its quills.

The porcupine's body is covered with sharp quills that are from two to twenty inches long. When an animal attacks, the porcupine strikes out. It runs sideways against the enemy. It swings at the attacker with the quills on its tail. The quills are not poisonous, but they do stick into the enemy's flesh.

It's *not* true that porcupines can "shoot" their quills at their enemies.

PORCUPINE

Hedgehogs are small. . . .

The biggest hedgehogs grow to be about one and a half feet long and weigh about three pounds.

Hedgehogs spend all their time on the ground. . . .

Hedgehogs live on the land in Europe, Asia, Africa, and New Zealand. They eat the insects, snakes, small animals, birds, and birds' eggs that they find on the ground.

. . . Porcupines are bigger.

Porcupines grow to be about twice as long (three feet long) and more than ten times as heavy (about 40 pounds).

. . . Some porcupines live in trees.

Old World porcupines also live in Europe, Asia, and Africa. They spend all their time on the ground. New World porcupines live in North and South America. They make their homes in pine and fir trees, where they eat the bark and leaves.

Some Final Words

You've just read about some famous animal mix-ups. Did you ever wonder why some animals can look alike and yet be different?

Scientists study —
— how animals have babies,
— how they breathe,
— how they move,
— the foods they eat,
— and so on.

Scientists group together all living things that are basically the same. They call this group a *kingdom.* All animals belong to the animal kingdom. All plants belong to the plant kingdom.

The animal kingdom is divided into smaller groups according to the way the animals look and act.

The next smaller group is called a *phylum.* As an example, all animals with a backbone belong in one phylum. This phylum includes dogs and cats, frogs and turtles, apes and humans. Animals without backbones belong to other phyla (plural of phylum).

Scientists divide each phylum into smaller groups according to other differences. Animals with backbones that give birth to living animals — such as dogs, cats, apes, and humans — go into one *class.* Animals with backbones that lay eggs — such as frogs and turtles — go into other classes.

Classes of animals are divided into even smaller groups according to still other differences. These groups are called *order, family, genus.*

Finally the groups are very small. Each has only one kind of animal and is called a *species.* One species may *look* similar to another, but as you've seen in this book, each species has characteristics that set it apart from the others. There are no important differences among members of the same species.

All human beings belong to one species. The species is *Homo sapiens.* Humans have babies, breathe, move, and eat the same way. Tall or short, fat or thin, fair or dark — we are all in the same species. No mix-ups here!